Collins

INTERNATIONAL PRIMARY ENGLISH
AS A SECOND LANGUAGE

Student's Book 2

Contents

About this book

This magazine-style Student's Book provides a wide variety of resources for classroom use and general enjoyment which act as the main stimulus (or "input") for the *Collins Cambridge Primary English as a Second Language* course. The modern presentation has been carefully designed to get learners interested and involved in the learning process and to provide stimuli for discussion. The main aim is to make language learning both engaging and enjoyable, and to get learners thinking about themselves and the exciting world they live in.

You will find stories, short information texts, poems, picture-dictionary pages, puzzles, simple graphs, as well as colourful illustrations and photographs linked to the topics for the year. The rich and varied visual resources provide interest and encourage oral communication and deeper thought about the topics.

Learners are guided through the material by clear, simple instructions which tell them what to read and give prompts for what else to do.

You will notice that there are coloured bubbles with small symbols on many of the pages.

This tells you that there is something to **talk** about.

This tells you that there is something to **think** about.

There are many opportunities for learners to talk about the materials. Talking should be encouraged and learners should not be afraid to talk about what they can see and what they have read and heard. Talking about their ideas allows them to use the language they are learning and improves their confidence and fluency. Sometimes they will need to use their mother tongue when sharing their ideas, experiences and deeper thoughts. This is a natural part of fluency development and should not be received negatively. Allow learners to express themselves fluently and confidently in their mother tongue, and then support them with the vocabulary they need to say it in English too!

Above all, learners should be enjoying their learning as this develops a positive and inquisitive approach to the world around them and their place within it.

The authors

Can you see me?

The students in Class 2 are taking photographs. One boy, called Ben, doesn't like being in photographs.

This is Ben. Can you see him in the photos?

Can you see me? I am next to the girl with a hat. Can you see Ben? He's got curly, red hair.

Can you see me? I have long hair. Can you see Ben?

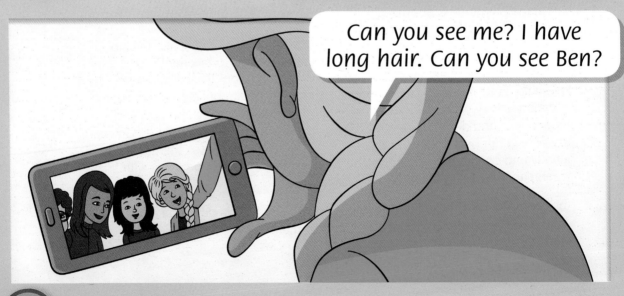

A Friend Helps

Look at the pictures. Listen to the story.

Thank you, Dove!

Crash!

Thank you, Ant. You're a good friend.

How do you help your friends?

On the street where I live

Where do you live? Who are your neighbours?

Look at the photographs of Amena's family, her neighbours and the picture of the street where they live.

My name's Amena. This is my family.

What is the name of the street?

Say the numbers of the houses.

These are our neighbours.

Looking at houses

Read the poem. Do you like the house?

My house

My house has ...
blue walls, white windows,
brown floors and red doors!

Look at the plan of a house. Work with a partner to ask and answer questions about this house.

bedroom

kitchen

bathroom

window

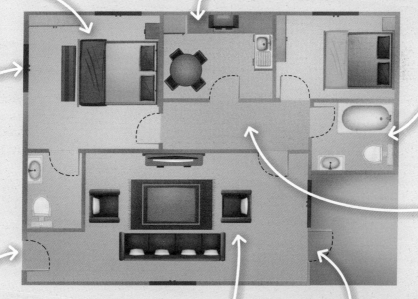

hallway

back door

front door

living room

The Three Goats

Look at the pictures. What is this story about?
Listen and follow the story.

Trip
trap
trip
trap!

Trip
trap
trip
trap!

Trip
trap
trip
trap!

CRASH!

Where did the giant live? Where do giants live in other stories you know?

Pirates

Look at the pictures. What is this story about?

Listen, then read the story.

A ship is a pirate's home. How is it different to your home?

1 Five big pirates went to the beach.

2 Four big pirates went to the river.

3 Three big pirates went to the trees.

4 Two big pirates went up the hill.

5 One big pirate went to the cave.

6 Five big pirates went back to the ship!

Palaces and castles

Read about different palaces and castles around the world.

Some people say "My home is my castle." Why?

The government of Mexico meets in this palace.

This is the palace of a traditional leader in Cameroon, in Africa.

The British Royal family live in Buckingham Palace.

Shah Jahan built this palace in India when his wife died.

This castle in France goes around a whole town. It protects the town.

In stories, princes and princesses live in castles like this one in Germany.

Who lives there?

Look at the photographs of different animals and where they live.
Read the information.

Lions and zebras live on the land.

Penguins live on the snow and ice.

Bats live in dark caves. So do bears.

These baby meerkats live in holes in the ground.

Bees live in beehives. They live in big groups.

Which other animal homes do you know?

Monkeys live in trees. So do birds and snakes.

It Was a Cold, Dark Night

Look at the pictures. What is this story about?
Listen, then read the story.

It was a cold, dark night and the wind was blowing.

Ned, the hedgehog, was looking for a home.
He looked down a little hole.

The rabbits said, "This is *our* home! Look next door."

He looked down a big hole.
The fox said, "This is *my* home! Look next door!"

He looked up in the tree.

The owls said, "Whoo-oo! This is *our* home. Look next door!"

5

The hedgehog looked up at the old barn. The bats said, "This is *our* home. But look down, Ned!"

6

Ned looked down and there was a big pile of leaves.

7

Ned said, "My home!" and he went to sleep all winter.

8

Different coats

**Look at the photographs.
Read the sentences.**

Ducks and eagles
have feathers.

We have skin. An elephant
has skin too.

Tortoises and
crabs have shells.

Bears and cats
have fur.

Sheep and goats
have wool.

Snakes and fish have scales.

Why do
animals have
different coats?

The Hare and the Tortoise

Look at the pictures. What is this story about?
Listen, then read the story.

Let's have a race.

Tortoise was slow. Hare was fast.

Hare ate carrots and he played.

Hare slept. Tortoise walked.

Then Hare ran fast.

But Tortoise won the race.

Why did Tortoise win the race?

The Lion and the Mouse

Look at the pictures. What is this story about?
Listen, then read the story.

1 A lion was sleeping.

The lion opened his eyes. **2**

3 He saw the mouse.

Got you!

Let me go! I'm so small.

4

Go away! Let me sleep.

5 The lion let the mouse go.

ROARRR!

The mouse saw the lion. He was in a net. **6**

The lion was free!

You are so small but you saved me. Thank you! **8**

7 The mouse bit the net.

Why did the mouse help the lion? Was the lion surprised?

Lions

**Look at the photographs.
Read the labels.
Compare the lions.**

ears

hair

A lion cub

whiskers

paws

claws

tail

How is the lion cub different to the adult lion?

mane

An adult male lion

Baby turtles

Read the labels in the the chart about the life of turtles.

The mother turtle lays eggs on the beach.

She covers the eggs with sand.

Baby turtles hatch from the eggs.

The baby turtles run to the sea.

Crabs and birds eat some of the baby turtles.

They return to the same beach to lay their eggs.

The baby turtles grow up in the sea.

Which other animals live both on the land and in the sea?

Food poems

Eating noodles

Stringy strips of noodles

Tasty tomato sauce

Twist them, turn them

In my mouth they go

And all over my shirt!

How do *you* eat noodles?

Mangoes are messy!

Carrots are crunchy

Coconuts are milky.

Pears are very tasty.

But mangoes are messy!

Raj Has a Good Idea

Look at the pictures. What is this story about? Read the story.

Where can you plant seeds?

Ada found a plastic bottle.

Raj had an idea.

Raj cut the bottle in half.

Then he made some holes.

He put the soil in the bottle and he planted some seeds.

"Do you have any soil?" he asked Ada.

What's Inside?

**Look at the photographs.
Answer the questions.**

What's inside the pod?

some peas

What's inside
the shell?

a walnut

What's inside
the mango?

a yolk

a big seed

sweet juice

What's inside
the eggshell?

What's inside
the orange?

a white

What's inside the
pomegranate?

lots of seeds

Can you
think of other types
of fruit with seeds
inside?

Pancakes

Read the recipe. Look at how to make the pancakes.

What can you put in the cooked pancakes?

You will need:

1½ cups of flour

1½ cups of milk

1 tablespoon of sugar

2 eggs

½ teaspoon of salt

2 tablespoons of melted butter (or oil)

What you do:

1. Mix the flour, sugar and salt in a bowl.

2. Add the eggs, butter and milk.

3. Beat the mixture.
4. Warm up a frying pan.

5. Put a little oil in the pan.
6. Put one spoon of mixture into the pan.

7. Let the pancake cook.
8. Turn it over and let the other side cook.

Jam and Yoghurt

Look at the pictures. What is this story about?
Listen, then read the story.

Are Easy to Make

Food from different places

Look at the pictures. Read about some foods from different countries.

pizza

This is a bread with cheese, tomato and olives. It is popular in most countries.

kimchi

This is cabbage mixed with onions, garlic, chilli and ginger. It is popular in Korea.

rice and peas

This dish has red beans and rice – but no peas! It is popular in the Caribbean.

feijoada

This is a stew with beans and meat. It is popular in Brazil.

Can you find Brazil and Korea on a map?

Which dishes are popular where you live?

Best Bird

Look at the pictures. What is this story about?
Read the story.

1. I'm the best bird.
2. I can fly. But I can dive.
3. I can hoot. But I can talk!
4. I can see a long way! But I can run fast!
5. I can hide among the leaves. But I can slide on the ice.
6. We're all best at something.

The cross-country race

Read the instructions. Play the game.

Start

1

2

3
You run fast.
Go forward
3 spaces.

4

Finish

30
You see the
finish line! Go
to FINISH.

FINISH

29

28

27
You lose a
shoe. Go back
3 spaces.

26

Dance to the Beat

Look at the pictures. Read about how to dance.

Can you dance?

1

First, you listen to the beat of the music.

2

Next, you skip around to the beat of the music.

3

Then you stamp your feet to the beat of the music.

4

Then you wave your arms to the beat of the music.

5

Now you clap your hands to the beat of the music. 6

You can shake your head to the beat of the music.

7

Stop when you hear the last beat of the music.

8

What do you do when you dance? How do you keep the beat?

What Will They Make?

Look at the pictures. What is the story about?
Read the story.

Mrs Matsuki's class are entering a competition. Each child will make something from paper.

What will you make, Rui?

You'll see!

What will you make, Sako?

You'll see!

What will you make, Mariko?

You'll see!

Taking part in a fun walk

Read the poster. How can you join the fun walk?

Can you walk fast?
Can you walk far?
Then why not enter our Fun Walk?

FUN WALK
4 kilometres

When: Saturday 2 April at 11:00
(Be there at 10.30.)

Where: In front of the Oakdale Secondary School, Dream Street.

Enter online: www.FUNWALKOAK.com

It's free and fun!
Everyone welcome.

Which fun activities or competitions have you heard about? Which would you like to enter?

Can it fly?

Listen and read the poems.

The incy wincy spider

The incy wincy spider
Climbed up the water spout.
Down came the rain
And washed the spider out.

Out came the sun
And dried up all the rain.
So the incy wincy spider
Climbed up the spout again.

The bird

Here are the legs
that walk along.

Here is the beak
that sings a song.

Here are the wings
that flap and spread.

And here is the bird
above my head.

by Tony Mitton

Most insects have wings

Look at the photographs and read about insects.

Insects are small animals.

They have 3 main body parts and 6 legs.

They have antennae and special eyes.

Most insects have wings.

Most insects hatch from eggs.

Some insects sting.

There are more than 6 million different insects on Earth.

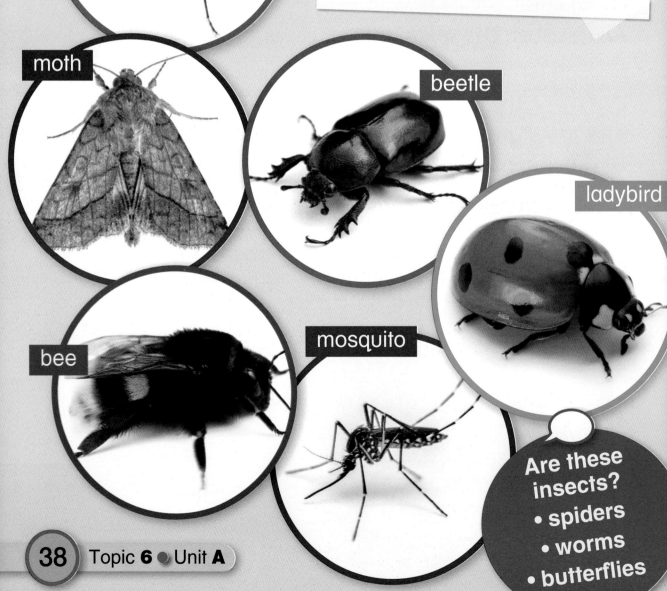

ant

moth

beetle

ladybird

bee

mosquito

Are these insects?
- spiders
- worms
- butterflies

The helper birds

Look at the photographs and read about birds that help other animals.

Oxpeckers are birds that like to eat ticks. They are sometimes called tickbirds. Tickbirds fly up and warn animals when there is danger.

Ticks are small animals. They suck blood from other animals and make their skin itchy.

Plovers are birds that are not afraid of crocodiles. They are like toothbrushes. They eat small bits of meat on the crocodile's teeth.

The Bird King

**Look at the pictures. What is this story about?
Listen, then read the story.**

All the land animals had
a king.

The birds did not have
a king.

The birds had a meeting.

Who can be
a good king?

The bird who
can fly high.

The birds had a race.

The birds flew up in the sky.

Some came down again.
They were tired.

Eagle said, "I can fly high and I am strong. I am the king."

But look! Who is that? It's Sparrow.

I am the king.

Eagle was very cross.

That is why Sparrow has a short tail.

Making a nest

Look at the photographs.
Read the information about
how birds make nests.

Weaver birds make
their own homes.

They weave grass, leaves
and twigs into a nest.

They make entrances
to the nests.

Can you think
of other animals that
build homes? What do
they use to make their
homes?

The nests hang from
the branches of trees.

Helicopters

Look at the photographs. Read the information.

Helicopters are small but they are very useful. They can fly anywhere. They can take off and land in very small places.

We can use helicopters to rescue people from mountains.

We can also use them to fight fires.

blade

engine

cockpit

tail rotor

landing skids

passenger seats

What else can we use a helicopter for?

The Magic Egg

**Look at the pictures. What is this story about?
Read the story.**

What do you sometimes wish for?

The Dolphin King

Read the story.

Jean and his friends were fishermen. Jean said, "I can throw a spear better than any of you." He hurled his spear at a dolphin.

The animal screamed and dived beneath the waves. Suddenly, a fierce storm blew up and it looked as though the boat might sink.

Then Jean and his friends saw a strange knight rising out of the waves. The knight shouted, "You nearly killed the dolphin king, and for this, you'll all drown."

Jean cried, "No, I alone threw the spear. Take me."
The knight carried Jean down to the bottom of the sea.

There, the dolphin king was waiting.

The knight whispered to Jean, "You must heal him."

Gently, Jean removed the spear and cleaned the wound.

The king opened his eyes and said, "Promise me that you and your friends will never hunt dolphins again."

Jean cried, "I promise."

The knight took him back to the boat. The storm had died and Jean's friends were saved.

Whales and dolphins die if they get caught in fishing nets. What can we do to protect them?

People who keep us safe

Read the information about people who keep us safe.

My parents look after me when I feel scared.

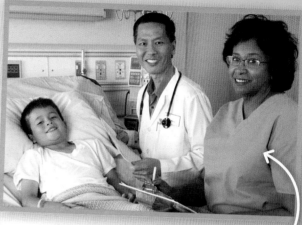

Nurses and doctors look after us when we are sick.

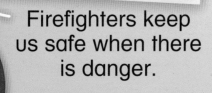

Firefighters keep us safe when there is danger.

Police officers keep us safe when we are out.

Who else helps to keep you safe?

What's that building?

Look at the pictures and answer the question.

What's that building?

It's a _____. It's where you _____.

Bank

RETAIL/OFFICE PREMISES
144.25m² (1,553ft²)

TO LET

Breakfast Menu

Coffee, Cappuccino, Latté or Orange juice

Scrambled eggs

Poached eggs

Cheese toastie

Cereal

Rebecca at the Funfair

Look at the pictures. What is this story about?
Listen, then read the story.

Hall of mirrors

Rebecca said, "Please! I want to do that!" 1

Rebecca looked thin, Rebecca looked fat. 2

Rebecca looked tall. Rebecca looked small. 3

Rebecca said, "Help! I don't like this at all." 4

Rebecca said, "Please!
5 Can I go around?"

Rebecca went up.
Rebecca went down.

6

Rebecca went green and
started to shout.

7

"Help!" said Rebecca.
"I want to get out!" **8**

Rebecca said, "Please! I want to do that!" 9

Rebecca got teddies. Rebecca got cats. 10

Rebecca got sweets and a big pink bear. 11

Rebecca said, "Yes! I *do* like the fair!" 12

Under your feet

Read about travelling underground.

Big cities are crowded. There are too many cars and buses, so many big cities have trains that go under the ground. These are sometimes called metros or subways. These trains can move around quickly under the ground. They move through special tunnels.

Why do people in London call the subway "the Tube"?

The subway in London is called the London Underground. People talk about going on the *Tube*.

PICCADILLY CIRCUS

Sounds

Look at the pictures. Read about sounds.

Hearing sounds

You hear sounds with your ears. There are sounds all around you.

bang

buzz

boom

hum

ding-dong

1

Which sounds do you like?

buzzz

♪

bbbbrrrrring!

SMASH

2

Making sounds

Sounds are made in many ways.

The clapper hits the bell and the bell makes a sound.

ring

bell

clapper

3

There are little bells and big bells.

A clock tower bell

A bicycle bell

4

The drumstick hits the drum and the drum makes a sound.

Drumstick

bang-bang-a boom!

drum

5

Some drums are big and some are small.

6

You pluck a string and it makes a sound.

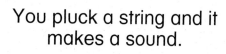

twang

7

toot
toot
toot

You blow into a recorder and it makes a sound.

8

Loud and soft sounds

Some sounds are soft …

whisper whisper

9

… and some sounds are loud.
Loud sounds can hurt your ears.

drrrrrr!

10

Sounds all around

Listen to the sounds around you.

Can you tell what's making them?

11

ROAR

pheep

12

What sounds do you like?
What sounds don't you like?

Sound poems

Read the poems then act them.

Sounds like me
Roar like a lion,
Squeak like a mouse.
Miaow like a cat
Locked out of the house.

Howl like a wolf,
Buzz like a bee.
Then shout, with your own voice,
Hello! This is me!

by Ian Larmont

My Big Band
"Ting" went the triangle.
"Foo" went the flute.
"Whee" went the whistle.
The horn went "Toot".
"Crash" went the cymbal.
"Boom" went the drum.
"Ta-ra" went the trumpet.
"Quiet!" yelled Mum.

by Tony Mitton

All sorts of music

Read about different musical instruments.

Violins have strings. You move a bow across the strings to make sounds.

These violinists are playing in an orchestra.

Steelpans are drums made of metal. They come from Trinidad and Tobago. These children are playing at a festival.

Didgeridoos come from Australia. You blow into the long pipe to make sounds. It is difficult to blow.

Xylophones have strips of wood or metal. You hit the strips with little hammers to make sounds.

Our Band

Look at the pictures. What is this story about?
Listen, then read the story.

"We should make our own band," said Lee. "I can play the drums."

Lee, Charlie and Maria loved music.

"OK. I can play the recorder," said Charlie, "and Maria can also play the recorder."

How many people do we need?" asked Lee.

"I don't know," said Maria.

Everyone wanted to join the band.

Soon there were 16 people in the band.

They had a concert at Lee's home. The families came to watch.

"Bravo!" said Lee's mom.

"Very good, but I think you need to practise!" said Maria's grandpa.

Would you like to play in a band? Why? Why not?

HarperCollins PUBLISHERS
Since 1817

William Collins' dream of knowledge for all began with the publication of his first book in 1819.
A self-educated mill worker, he not only enriched millions of lives, but also founded a flourishing publishing house. Today, staying true to this spirit, Collins books are packed with inspiration, innovation and practical expertise. They place you at the centre of a world of possibility and give you exactly what you need to explore it.

Collins. Freedom to teach.

An imprint of HarperCollins*Publishers*
The News Building
1 London Bridge Street
London SE1 9GF

browse the complete Collins catalogue at
www.collins.co.uk

© HarperCollins*Publishers* Limited 2017

10 9 8 7 6 5 4 3 2 1

ISBN 978-0-00-821361-9

Daphne Paizee asserts her moral right to be identified as the author of this work.

British Library Cataloguing in Publication Data
A catalogue record for this publication is available from the British Library.

Publisher Celia Wigley
Commissioning editor Karen Jamieson
Series editor Karen Morrison
Managing editor Sarah Thomas
Editor Alexander Rutherford
Project managed by Tara Alner
Edited by Tracy Thomas
Proofread by Zoe Smith
Cover design by ink-tank and associates
Cover artwork by QBS
Internal design by Ken Vail Graphic Design
Typesetting by Ken Vail Graphic Design
Illustrations by QBS
Production by Lauren Crisp

Printed and bound by Grafica Veneta S. P. A.

MIX
Paper from
responsible sources
FSC www.fsc.org **FSC™ C007454**

FSC™ is a non-profit international organisation established to promote the responsible management of the world's forests. Products carrying the FSC label are independently certified to assure consumers that they come from forests that are managed to meet the social, economic and ecological needs of present and future generations, and other controlled sources.

Find out more about HarperCollins and the environment at
www.harpercollins.co.uk/green

Text acknowledgements
The publishers gratefully acknowledge the permissions granted to reproduce copyright material in the book. Every effort has been made to contact the holders of copyright material, but if any have been inadvertently overlooked, the Publisher will be pleased to make the necessary arrangements at the first opportunity.

Poem on p37, 'The Bird' by Tony Mitton first published in Finger Rhymes, compiled by John Forster and illustrated by Carol Thompson, OUP UK 1996 with permission from David Higham Associates Ltd; Poem on p60, 'Sounds like me', by Ian Larmont in Oxford Reading Tree: Levels 3-4: Glow-worms: Sounds Poems, compiled by John Foster © Ian Larmont 1995; Poem on p60, 'My Big Band' by Tony Mitton first published in Sounds, published by OUP © Tony Mitton 1995 with permission from David Higham Associates Ltd

HarperCollins*Publishers* Limited for extracts and artwork from:

Pirates by Paul Shipton, illustrated by Kelly Waldek, text © 2005 Paul Shipton. It Was a Cold, Dark Night by Tim Hopgood, illustrated by Tim Hopgood, text © 2010 Tim Hopgood. The Hare and the Tortoise by Melanie Williamson, illustrated by Melanie Williamson, text © 2013 Melanie Williamson. The Lion and the Mouse by Anthony Robinson, illustrated by Ciaran Duffy, text © 2011 Anthony Robinson. The Baby Turtle by Andy & Angie Belcher, text © 2007 Andy & Angie Belcher. Best Bird by Laura Hambleton, illustrated by Laura Hambleton, text © 2011 Laura Hambleton. Dance to the Beat by Uz Afzal, text © 2005 Uz Afzal. Helper Bird by Anita Ganeri, text © 2011 Anita Ganeri. The Magic Egg by Vivian French, illustrated by Karen Donnelly, text © 2010 Vivian French. The Dolphin King by Saviour Pirotta, illustrated by Fausto Bianchi, text © 2012 Saviour Pirotta. Rebecca at the Funfair by Frances Ridley, illustrated by Teri Gower, text © 2005 Frances Ridley. Sounds by Julie Sykes, text © 2005 Julie Sykes.

Photo acknowledgements
The publishers wish to thank the following for permission to reproduce photographs. Every effort has been made to trace copyright holders and to obtain their permission for the use of copyright materials. The publishers will gladly receive any information enabling them to rectify any error or omission at the first opportunity.

(t = top, c = centre, b = bottom, r = right, l = left, Ss = Shutterstock)

Cover & p1 QBS

p8t ZouZou/Ss, p8b michaeljung/Ss, p9 Vector House/Ss, p12tl Frontpage/Ss, p12tr Art Directors & TRIP/Alamy, p12cl r.nagy/Ss, p12cr turtix/Ss, p12bl javarman/Ss, p12br canadastock/Ss, p13 Vidoslava/Ss, p13t Felix Lipov/Ss, p13tl BMJ/Ss, p13tr Weblogiq/Ss, p13bl KAMONRAT/Ss, p13br PCHT/Ss, p13b Svetlana Romantsova/Ss, p16 sdecoret/Ss, p16tl1 GUNDAM_Ai/Ss, p16tl2 E. O./Ss, p16tr1 gdvcom/Ss, p16tr2 Greg and Jan Ritchie/Ss, p16cl1 Zhiltsov Alexandr/Ss, p16cl2 Reinhold Leitner/Ss, p16cr1 Alta Oosthuizen/Ss, p16cr2 aodaodaodaod/Ss, p16bl1 reptiles4all/Ss, p16bl2 Andreas Gradin/Ss, p16br1 Olha Rohulya/Ss, p16br2 Images by Dr. Alan Lipkin/Ss, p20t Stuart G Porter/Ss, p20b PHOTOCREO Michal Bednarek/Ss, p21tl David Evison/Ss, p21tc Andy and Angie Belcher, p21tr Alamy/Aqua Image, p21bl Maja Nicht/Ss, p21bl1 akhnyushchy/Ss, p21bl2 APHITHANA/Ss, p21c foryouinf/Ss, p21br Andy and Angie Belcher, p21bc Dai Mar Tamarack/Ss, p22t oekka.k/Ss, p22bl Viktar Malyshchyts/Ss, p22br witty234/Ss, p24tl Luiscar74/Ss, p24tr Brilliance stock/Ss, p24cl Mr.Nakorrn/Ss, p24cr Kovaleva_Ka/Ss, p24bl EM Arts/Ss, p24br Bocos Benedict/Ss, p25tl OlgaHomka/Ss, p25br MarijaPiliponyte/Ss, p25 Valentin Chemyakin/Ss, p28tl svry/Ss, p28tr Kongsak/Ss, p28bl Paul_Brighton/Ss, p28br rocharibeiro/Ss, p32 In-Finity/Ss, p32 Steve Lumb, p36 ekler/Ss, p37l natixa/Ss, p38t infocus/Ss, p38cl EEO/Ss, p38cr Worraket/Ss, p38bl Vova Shevchuk/Ss, p38bc Akil Rolle-Rowan/Ss, p38br Valentina Proskurina/Ss, p39t rugco/Ss, p39c enrik Larsson/Ss, p39b Juniors Bildarchiv/Alamy, p43tr Utopia_88/Ss, p43tl Tobie Oosthuizen/Ss, p43br Four Oaks/Ss, p43bl Glass and Nature/Ss, p44tl corlaffra/Ss, p44tr Yongyut Kumsri/Ss, p44bl Digital Media Pro/Ss, p44br Whitevector/Ss, p51tl pixelheadphoto digitalskillet/Ss, p51tr Monkey Business Images/Ss, p51bl Tatiana Belova/Ss, p51br Paolo Bona/Ss, p52tl Samuel Borges Photography/Ss, p52tr Ronnachai Palas/Ss, p52cl Capricorn Studio/Ss, p52c Mark William Richardson/Ss, p52cr Stephen Coburn/Ss, p52bl Lorenzo Patoia/Ss, p52br Vladimir Wrangel /Ss, p56t Danilovski/Ss, p56b upungato/Ss, p57-59 Martin Sookias, p57tc Irina Diculescu/Ss, p57tr Bachkova Natalia/Ss, p57c TZIDO SUN/Ss, p57cr W. Scott McGill/Ss, p57bc Arterra Picture Library/Alamy, p57br oley/Ss, p58c xdyl/Ss, p58br legDoroshin/Ss, p60 Richard Laschon/Ss, p60t ffoto29/Ss, p60b GraphicsRF/Ss, p61tl John de la Bastide/Ss, p61tr Blulz60/Ss, p61bl PK.pawaris/Ss, p61br usan Montgomery/Ss